ABC
at the Shops

Rebecca Rissman

Raintree

www.raintreepublishers.co.uk
Visit our website to find out more information about Raintree books.

To order:
☎ Phone 0845 6044371
🖷 Fax +44 (0) 1865 312263
🖳 Email myorders@raintreepublishers.co.uk

Customers from outside the UK please telephone +44 1865 312262

Raintree is an imprint of Capstone Global Library Limited, a company incorporated in England and Wales having its registered office at 7 Pilgrim Street, London, EC4V 6LB – Registered company number: 6695582

Text © Capstone Global Library Limited 2013
First published in hardback in 2013
The moral rights of the proprietor have been asserted.

Edited by Dan Nunn and Rebecca Rissman
Designed by Joanna Hinton-Malivoire
Picture research by Ruth Blair
Originated by Capstone Global Library Ltd
Production by Alison Parsons
Printed in China by South China Printing Company Ltd

ISBN 978 1 406 24086 3
16 15 14 13 12
10 9 8 7 6 5 4 3 2 1

British Library Cataloguing in Publication Data
Rissman, Rebecca.
ABC at the shops. – (Everyday alphabet)
428.1'3-dc23
A full catalogue record for this book is available from the British Library.

Acknowledgements
We would like to thank the following for permission to reproduce photographs: Dreamstime.com p. 9 (© Monkey Business Images); Shutterstock pp. 4 (© Feng Yu), 5 (© atoss), 6 (© Studio DMM Photography, Designs & Art), 7 (© Zayats Svetlana), 8 (© Inc), 10 (© Alexander Dashewsky), 11 (© Petrenko Andriy), 12 (© Elena Elisseeva), 13 (© Rafa Irusta), 14 (© atoss), 15 (© Valentyn Volkov), 16 (© Peter zijlstra), 17 (© Andrjuss), 18 (© GeorgeS), 19 (© Kamenetskiy Konstantin), 20 (© jreika), 21 (© Janet Faye Hastings), 22 (© Shmeliova Natalia), 23 (© valzan), 24 (© TerraceStudio), 25 (© liza1979), 26 (© Elena Schweitzer), 27 (© Mikus, Jo.), 28 (© Lepas), 29 (© atoss), 30 (© graja, © Michael Cocita), 31 (© Valentyn Volkov, © Loskutnikov, © Tim Arbaev).

Cover photograph of food in a supermarket aisle reproduced with permission of Shutterstock (© Hannamariah).

Every effort has been made to contact copyright holders of any material reproduced in this book. Any omissions will be rectified in subsequent printings if notice is given to the publisher.

Contents

Aa

asparagus

Asparagus is a tasty vegetable you can buy in a shop. Eating asparagus helps you stay healthy.

B b

bananas

Bananas are often green when you buy them. When bananas are ripe, they turn yellow.

Cc

crayons

Coloured crayons are great for drawing pictures. What picture can you draw?

Dd

doll

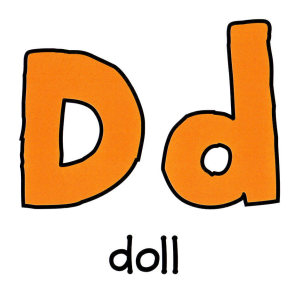

You can buy lots of different dolls. There are rag dolls, baby dolls, tiny dolls, and many more.

7

Ee

eggs

Hens lay eggs. Then the eggs are sold in boxes.

Ff

flour

Flour is used in baking. We use it to make bread, biscuits, and cakes.

G g

grapes

Grapes are fruit. You can buy green and purple grapes.

10

Hh

honey

Honey is made by bees!
Shops sell it in jars.
Honey tastes great
on toast.

11

Ii

ice cream

Ice cream is made from milk. You can eat ice cream scoops on tasty cones.

Jj

juice

Juice can be made from oranges, apples, grapes, and many other fruits. Juice tastes great!

kiwi fruit

Kiwi fruit have brown, fuzzy skin, but their insides taste sweet!

Ll

lemons

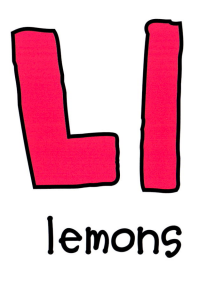

Lemons are fruit that grow on trees. Lemons taste very sour!

M m

mangoes

Mangoes are fruit with a thick skin and a big seed. Mangoes taste very sweet.

16

Nn

nectarines

Nectarines are fruit with a large, hard seed. This is why they are sometimes called "stone fruit"!

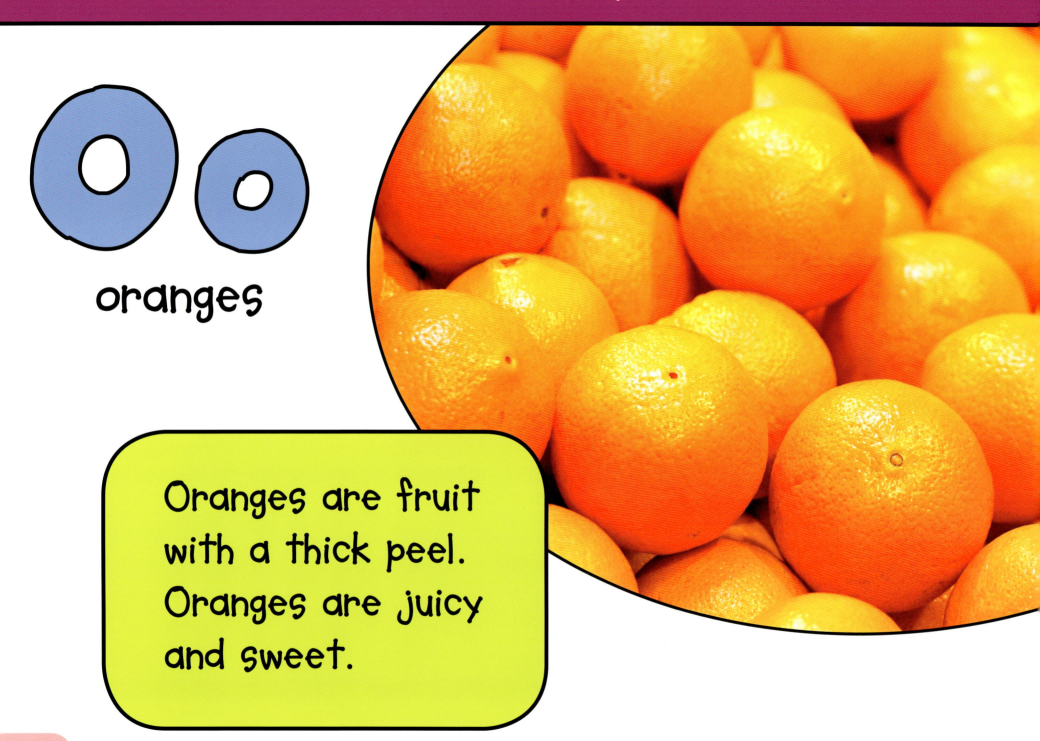

oranges

Oranges are fruit with a thick peel. Oranges are juicy and sweet.

18

P p

potatoes

Potatoes are vegetables that grow under the ground. Crisps are made from potatoes.

Qq

quiches

Quiches are egg pies! You can buy quiches at some shops to take home and eat.

Rr

raspberries

Raspberries are small red berries. They are very sweet and have many little seeds.

21

Ss

shoes

Shoes are made in all shapes, sizes, and colours. You buy two shoes in a pair.

Tt

tomatoes

Tomatoes are round, red fruit. They are used to make pasta sauce, and ketchup.

23

Uu

umbrella

Don't forget your umbrella if you go shopping on a rainy day!

vegetables

Eating vegetables keeps you healthy. What are your favourite vegetables?

25

Ww

watermelons

Watermelons are large fruit. They have a thick green rind on the outside and red flesh on the inside.

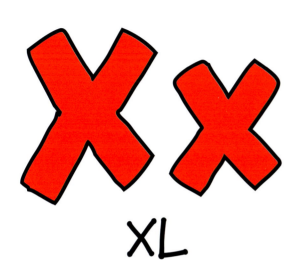

XL

T-shirts come in different sizes. XL stands for "extra large".

27

yogurt

Yogurt is a food made from milk. You can buy it in different flavours.

Zz

zucchinis

Zucchini is another word for "courgette". They say "zucchini" instead of courgette in America.

29

Find your own ABC at the shops

Can you find your own ABC at the shops? How many different things beginning with each letter can you find? Here are some ideas to help you!

Mm

Rr

Tt

31

Index